To: _____

From: _____

Published by Sellers Publishing, Inc.
Text and illustrations copyright © 2011 Sandy Gingras

Sellers Publishing, Inc.
161 John Roberts Road, South Portland, Maine 04106
Visit our Web site: www.sellerspublishing.com
E-mail: rsp@rsvp.com

ISBN 13: 978-1-4162-0647-7

10 9 8 7 6 5 4 3 2

Printed and bound in China.

LOVE is...

by Sandy Gingras

SELLERS
PUBLISHING

"How do I Love Thee?
Let me count The ways."

-Elizabeth Barrett Browning

Love is
putting our hearts
on The Line

Love is...

playing footsie

Love is...

when we don't push
each other's buttons
(although we know
where they are).

Love is

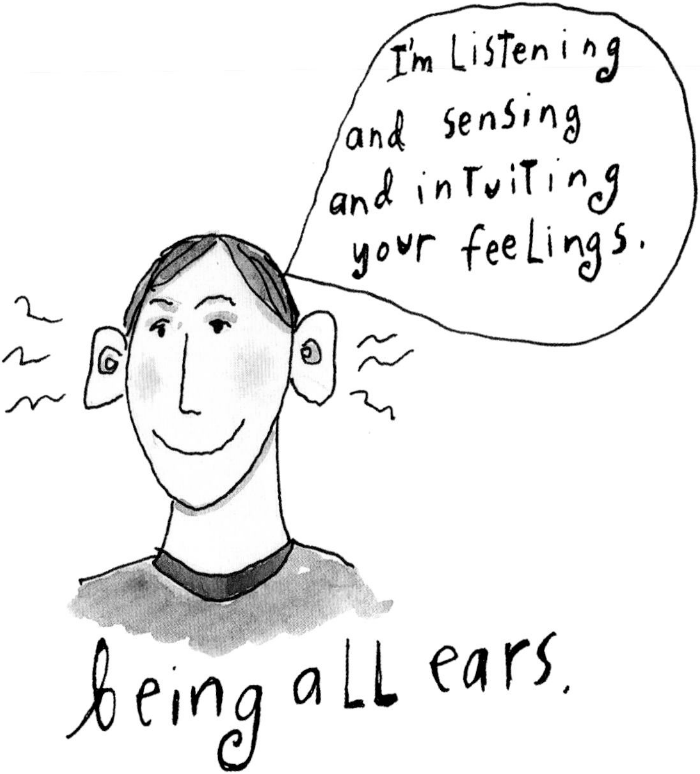

being all ears.

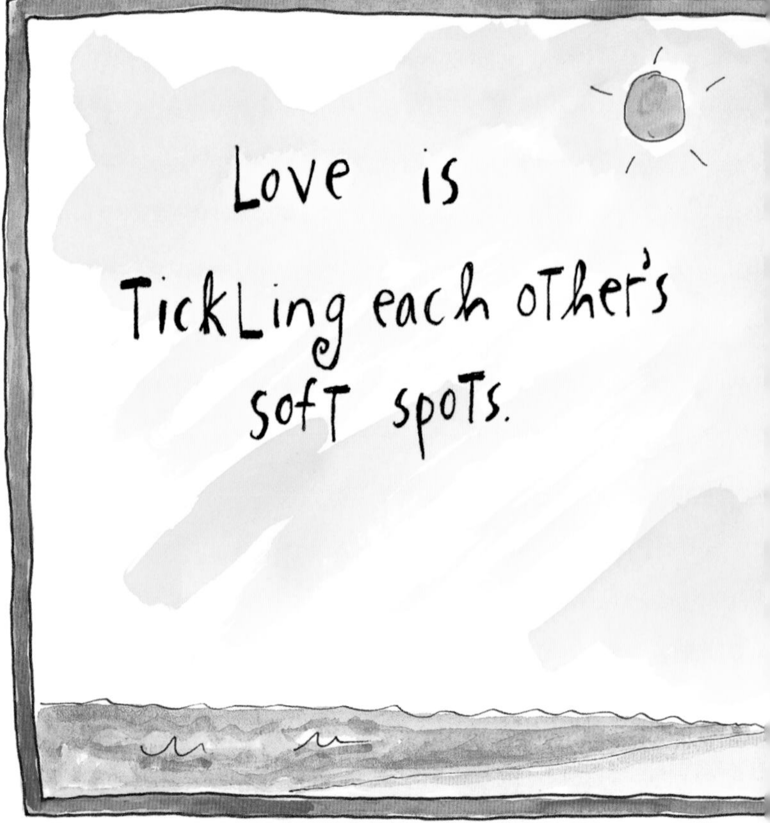
Love is
TickLing each other's
soft spots.

Love is
forgiving
and forgetting

Love is

Smoochey

Smoochey

Smoochey

Love is

You are my duck,
my bunny, my Lambkin,
my pet, my kitten,
my fuzzy wuzzy bear...

Love is
animal

Love is

Love is

number 1

our first kiss

Vive La difference

Love is...

endurance

Love is
showing
our True coLors

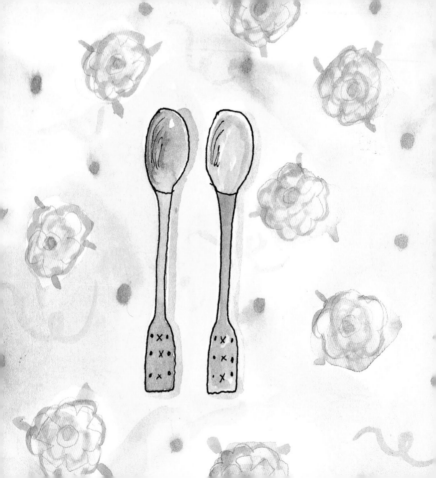

Love is

fitting together

Like spoons

Love is
supporting each other's
crazy LiTTLe
dreams

"If you would only change the way you dress and the way you chew your food and those friends that you have, if you would just part your hair on the side and drive slower and not say silly things anymore, if you would not slurp your soup and leave the shower dripping and, by the way, could you not wear that T-shirt anymore, and stop putting

Love is
acceptance

Love is

a dance

Love is
being on
each other's
side.

Love is
opening up

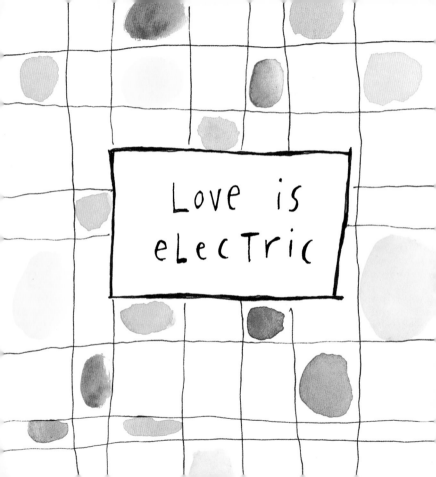

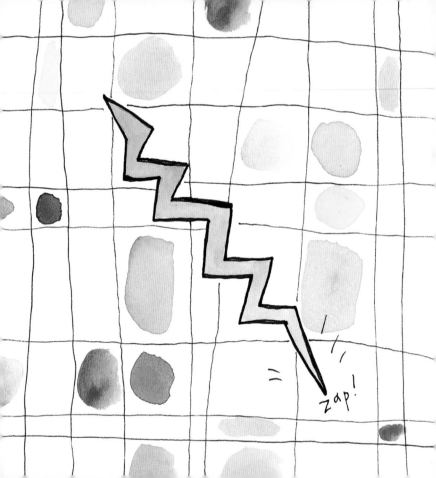

Love is
meeTing
in The middle

Love is

a good back rub

Love is...

once
upon
a
time

TeLLing and re-TeLLing
The story of how
we meT.

a big umbrella
on a rainy day.

Love is...

keeping things
spicy

Love is
reciprocal

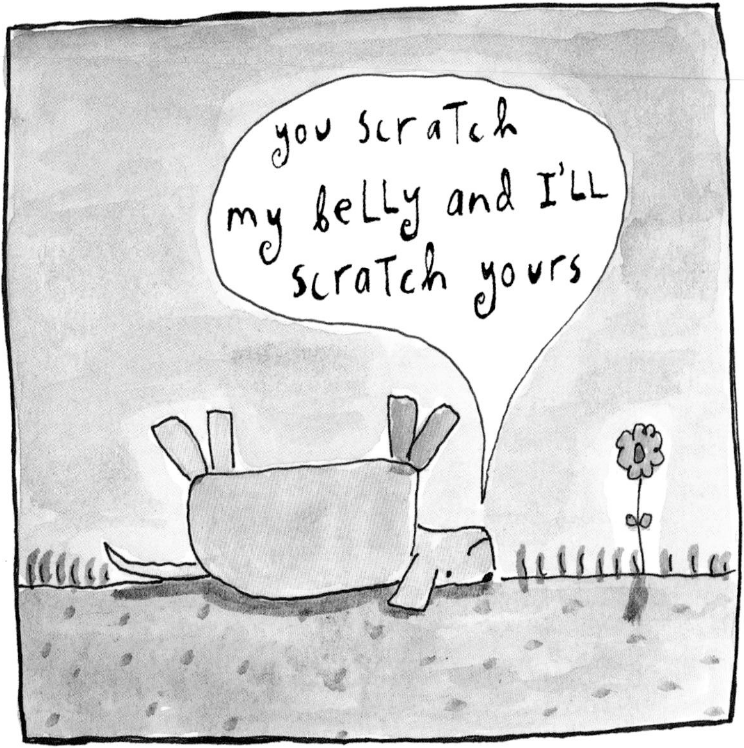
you scratch my belly and I'll scratch yours